THE BOOK OF
FINANCIAL WISDOM

BY
C. FOSTER STANBACK

ILLUSTRATED BY
JONATHAN STANBACK

Published by Lulu®
www.lulu.com

Printed in the United States of America

ISBN-978-1-105-09899-4

Table of Contents

Preface

By three methods we may learn wisdom: First, by reflection, which is noblest; Second, by imitation, which is easiest; and third, by experience, which is the bitterest. – Confucius

The financial wisdom that has been collected within the pages of this book finds its source in the great thinkers who have indeed followed Confucius' noblest path. The author has compiled their sayings with the goal of pointing out the easiest pathway to financial wellbeing, so that the bitter road of experience can be avoided.

– C. Foster Stanback

Work

Lazy hands make a man poor, but diligent hands bring wealth. – King Solomon (Pr 10:4)

He who works his land will have abundant food, but he who chases fantasies lacks judgement. – King Solomon (Pr 12:11)

The plans of the diligent lead to profit as surely as haste leads to poverty. – King Solomon (Pr 21:5)

Diligent hands will rule, but laziness ends in slave labor. – King Solomon (Pr 12:24)

The sluggard craves and gets nothing, but the desires of the diligent are fully satisfied. – King Solomon (Pr 13:4)

All hard work brings a profit, but mere talk leads to poverty. – King Solomon (Pr 14:23)

The laborer's appetite works for him; his hunger drives him on. – King Solomon (Pr 16:26)

Do you see a man skilled in his work? He will serve before kings; he will not serve before obscure men. – King Solomon (Pr 22:29)

One who is slack in his work is brother to one who destroys. – King Solomon (Pr 18:9)

Do not love sleep or you will grow poor; stay awake and you will have food to spare. – King Solomon (Pr 20:13)

Never fear the want of business. A man who qualifies himself well for his calling never fails of employment. – Thomas Jefferson

Folks who never do any more than they are paid for never get paid more than they do. – Elbert Hubbard

Sorrow's best antidote is employment. – Young

Without rest, a man cannot work; without work, the rest does not give you any benefit. – Abkhasian Proverb

The true wealth of a state consists in the number of its inhabitants, in their toil and industry. – Napoleon Bonaparte

He that will not work according to his faculty, let him perish according to his necessity: There is no law juster than that. – Thomas Carlyle

For even when we were with you, we gave you this rule: "If a man will not work, he shall not eat." – The Apostle Paul (2 Thessalonians 3:10)

You don't get paid for the hour. You get paid for the value you bring to the hour. – Jim Rohn

Nothing is so fatiguing as the eternal hanging on of an uncompleted task. – William James

We work to become, not to acquire. – Elbert Hubbard

You cannot change your destination overnight, but you can change your direction overnight. – Jim Rohn

You may know for a certainty that if your work is becoming uninteresting, so are you; for work is an inanimate thing and can be made lively and interesting only by injecting yourself into it. Your job is only as big as you are. – George C. Hubbs

I believe in work, hard work and long hours of work. Men do not break down from overwork, but from worry and dissipation. – Charles Evans Hughes

Amatuers hope; professionals work. – Garson Kanin

Those who have most to do, and are willing to work, will find the most time. – Samuel Smiles

The way to win is to work, work, work, work, and hope to have a few insights. – Charlie Munger

If you want to leave your footprints on the sands of time, be sure you're wearing work shoes. – Italian Proverb

Choose a job you love, and you will never have to work a day in your life. – Confucius

People forget how fast you did a job—but they remember how well you did it. – Howard W. Newton

It is easier to do a job right than to explain why you didn't. – Martin Van Buren

You cannot create prosperity by law. Sustained thrift, industry, application, intelligence are the only things that ever do, or will, create prosperity. But you can very easily destroy prosperity by law. – Theodore Roosevelt.

Extend pity to no man because he has to work. If he is worth his salt, he will work. I envy the man who has work worth doing and does it well. There never has been devised, and there never will be devised, any law which will enable a man to succeed save by the exercise of those qualities which have always been the prerequisites of success, the qualities of hard work, of keen intelligence, of unflinching will. – Theodore Roosevelt

Far and away the best prize that life offers is the chance to work hard at work worth doing. – Theodore Roosevelt

Lampis the shipowner, on being asked how he acquired great wealth, replied, "My great wealth was acquired with no difficulty, but my small wealth, my first gains, with much labor." – Epictetus

Some are bent with toil, and some get crooked trying to avoid it. – Herbert V. Prochnow

The highest reward for a person's toil is not what he gets for it, but what he becomes by it. – John Ruski

The world is moved not only by the mighty shoves of the heroes, but also by the aggregate of the tiny pushes of each honest worker. – Frank C. Ross

Work is often the father of pleasure. – Voltaire

Among a democratic people, where there is no hereditary wealth, every man works to earn a living, or is born of parents who have worked. The notion of labor is therefore presented to the mind, on every side, as the necessary, natural, and honest condition. – Alexis De Tocqueville

Work is the true elixir of life. The busiest man is the happiest man. Excellence in any art or profession is attained only by hard and persistent work. Never believe that you are perfect. When a man imagines, even after years of striving, that he has attained perfection, his decline begins. – Sir Theodore Martin

Labor disgraces no man; unfortunately, you occasionally find men who disgrace labor. – Ulysses S. Grant

Unless the job means more than the pay, it will never pay more. – H. Bertram Lewis

Thank God every morning when you get up that you have something to do that day which must be done, whether you like it or not. Being forced to work, and forced to do your best, will breed in you temperance and self-control, diligence and strength of will, cheerfulness and content, and a hundred virtues which the idle never know. – Charles Kingsley

I never remember feeling tired by work, though idleness exhausts me completely. – Sir Arthur Conan Doyle

No horse gets anywhere until he is harnessed. No steam or gas ever drives anything until it is confined. No Niagara is ever turned into light and power until it is tunneled. No life ever grows great until it is focused, dedicated, disciplined. – Harry Emerson Fosdick, D.D.

Nothing is really work unless you would rather be doing something else. – Chub De Wolfe

There is honor in labor. Work is the medicine of the soul. It is more: it is your very life, without which you would amount to little. – Grenville Kleiser

If you are poor, work. If you are burdened with seemingly unfair responsibilities, work. If you are happy, work. Idleness gives room for doubts and fears. If disappointments come, keep right on working. If sorrow overwhelms you and loved ones seem not true, work. If health is threatened, work. When faith falters and reason fails, just work. When dreams are shattered and hope seems dead, work. Work as if your life were in peril. It really is. No matter what ails you, work. Work faithfully— work with faith. Work is the greatest remedy available for both mental and physical afflictions. – Korsaren

We are not here to play, to dream, to drift;
We have hard work to do and loads to lift;
Shun not the struggle—face it,
'tis God's gift. – Lord Shaftesbury

If you have genius, industry will improve it; if you have none, industry will supply its place. – Sir Joshua Reynolds

All growth depends upon activity. There is no development physically or intellectually without effort, and effort means work. Work is not a curse; it is the prerogative of intelligence, the only means to manhood, and the measure of civilization. – Calvin Coolidge

This one makes a net;
This one stands and wishes.
Would you like to bet
Which one gets the fishes? – Chinese Rhyme

Don't be misled into believing that somehow the world owes you a living. The boy who believes that his parents, or the government, or anyone else owes him his livelihood and that he can collect it without labor will wake up one day and find himself working for another boy who did not have that belief and, therefore, earned the right to have others work for him. – David Sarnoff

The test of a vocation is the love of the drudgery it involves. – Logan Pearsall Smith

That some should be rich shows that others may become rich, and hence is just encouragement to industry and enterprise. – Abraham Lincoln

If you intend to go to work, there is no better place than right where you are; if you do not intend to go to work, you cannot get along anywhere. Squirming and crawling about from place to place can do no good. – Abraham Lincoln

Things may come to those who wait, but only the things left by those who hustle. – Abraham Lincoln

The prudent, penniless beginner in the world labors for wages for a while, saves a surplus with which to buy tools or land for himself for another while, and at length hires a new beginner to help him. This is the just and generous and prosperous system which opens the way to all, gives hope to all, and consequently energy and progress and improvement of conditions to all. – Abraham Lincoln

For me, hard work represents the supreme luxury of life. – Albert M. Greenfield

Man must work. That is certain as the sun. But he may work grudgingly or he may work gratefully; he may work as a man, or he may work as a machine. There is no work so rude that he may not exalt it; no work so impassive that he may not breathe a soul into it; no work so dull that he may not enliven it. – Henry Giles

The only time some people work like a horse is when the boss rides them. – Gabriel Heatte

Sloth makes all things difficult, but industry all things easy. – Benjamin Franklin

Industry need not wish, and he that lives upon hopes will die fasting. There are no gains without pains. He that hath a trade hath an estate, and he that hath a calling hath an office of profit and honor; but then the trade must be worked at, and the calling followed, or neither the estate nor the office will enable us to pay our taxes. If we are industrious, we shall never starve; for at the workingman's house hunger looks in, but dares not enter. Nor will the bailiff or the constable enter, for industry pays debts, while idleness and neglect increase them. – Benjamin Franklin

Good for the body is the work of the body, good for the soul is the work of the soul, and good for either is the work of the other. – Henry David Thoreau

The dignity of labor depends not on what you do, but how you do it. – Edwin Osgood Grover

Do not waste a minute—not a second—in trying to demonstrate to others the merits of your performance. If your work does not vindicate itself, you cannot vindicate it. – Thomas W. Higginson

Many times a day I realize how my own outer and inner life is built upon the labors of my fellow men, both living and dead, and how earnestly I must exert myself to return as much as I have received. – Albert Einstein

If we go far enough back into basic economics, we are eventually reminded that the only known way of producing money initially is by labor; somebody has to work with his brains or his back, and that capital is nothing more than the accumulation of money which has been paid to reward a man for his labor. – Walter B. Wriston

There is not, never has been, and never will be any substitute for productive work. No amount of legislation, no amount of money, borrowed or coined, no economic prestidigitation, governmental or otherwise, can, as such, increase by one iota the wealth of a nation or the standard of living of a people. Existing wealth or property can be and is being redistributed by law, but new wealth can be created only by men and by the man-made machines they guide. – Philip D. Reed

Genius begins great works; labor alone finishes them. – Joseph Joubert

Work is a great blessing; after evil came into the world, it was given as an antidote, not as a punishing. – Arthur S. Hardy

My grandfather once told me that there are two kinds of people: those who do the work and those who take the credit. He told me to try to be in the first group; there was much less competition there. – Indira Gandhi

The object of living is work, experience, happiness. There is joy in work. All that money can do is buy us someone else's work in exchange for our own. There is no happiness except in the realization that we have accomplished something. – Henry Ford

There are two ways of making yourself stand out from the crowd. One is by having a job so big you can go home before the bell rings if you want to. The other is by finding so much to do that you must stay after the others have gone. The one who enjoys the former once took advantage of the latter. – Henry Ford

He who does nothing renders himself incapable of doing anything; but while we are executing any work, we are preparing and qualifying ourselves to undertake another. – William Hazlitt

Employment is nature's physician, and is essential to human happiness. – Galen

They must hunger in frost that will not work in heat. – John Heywood

The right man can make a good job out of any job. – William Feather

If you have a job without any aggravations, you don't have a job. – Malcom Forbes

What Kind of a Chap Are You

Are you one of the chaps who can take his raps
And still not hit the floor;
Who'll stick by the gun till his task is done
And then look 'round for more?
Do you grin at your work or sulk and shirk
When the job seems hard to do;
Are you there with the grit to do your bit;
Can the boss depend on you?
Is your conscience clear, with nothing to fear
As you punch the clock each night;
When you leave the job, do your pulses throb
With the thought of a task done right?
Is it pleasure or dread when you pillow your head
And think of the coming day;
Do you breathe a prayer for strength to bear
Does your job mean simply play?
Just pause a bit and see if you fit
In the class that's pictured here—
For it's never too late to clean the slate
And start on a record clear. – Frank A. Collins

Running a Business

Drive thy business, or it will drive thee. – Benjamin Franklin

In a difficult business, no sooner is one problem solved than another surfaces—never is there just one cockroach in the kitchen. – Warren Buffett

All too often, we've seen value stagnate in the presence of hubris or boredom that caused the attention span of managers to wander. Would you believe that not a few decades back they were growing shrimp at Coke and exploring for oil at Gillette? – Warren Buffett

Just as work expands to fill available time, corporate projects or acquisitions will materialize to soak up available funds...any business craving of the leader, however foolish, will be quickly supported by detailed rate-of-return and strategic studies prepared by the troops. – Warren Buffett

A good managerial record (measured by economic returns) is far more a function of what business boat you get into than it is of how effectively you row. Should you find yourself in a chronically-leaking boat, energy devoted to changing vessels is likely to be more productive than energy devoted to patching leaks. – Warren Buffett

Can you really explain to a fish what it's like to walk on land? One day on land is worth a thousand years of talking about it, and one day running a business has exactly the same kind of value. – Warren Buffett

The managers at fault periodically report on the lesson they have learned from the latest disappointment. They then usually seek out future lessons. – Warren Buffett

In the business world, the rear view mirror is always clearer than the windshield. – Warren Buffett

When a management with a reputation for brilliance tackles a business with a reputation for bad economics, it is the reputation of the business that remains intact. – Warren Buffett

Understanding how to be a good investor makes you a better business manager and vice versa. – Charlie Munger

Choose clients as you would friends. – Charlie Munger

I do not believe maximizing profits for the investors is the only acceptable justification for all corporate actions. The investors are not the only people who matter. Corporations can exist for purposes other than simply maximizing profits. – John Mackey

Light is the task where many share the toil. – Homer

Never try to work a man who will work you to death trying to work him. – Robert Louis Wilson

Sweat equity has created far more billion-dollar companies than venture capital has. – Mark Cuban

Pay your people the least possible and you'll get from them the same. – Malcom Forbes

It marks a big step in a man's development when he comes to realize that other men can be called in to help him do a better job than he can do alone. – Andrew Carnegie

Take my assets—but leave me my organization and in five years I'll have it all back. – Alfred M. Sloan

There is one rule for industrialists and that is: Make the best quality of goods possible at the lowest cost possible, paying the highest wages possible. – Henry Ford

You can employ men and hire hands to work for you, but you will have to win their hearts to have them work with you. – William J.H. Boetcker

No matter how much work a man can do, no matter how engaging his personality may be, he will not advance far in business if he cannot work through others. – John Craig

We would rather have one man or woman working with us than three merely working for us. – J. Dabney Day

Saving

Dishonest money dwindles away, but he who gathers money little by little makes it grow. – King Solomon (Pr 13:11)

In the house of the wise are stores of choice food and oil, but a foolish man devours all he has. – King Solomon (Pr 21:20)

A nation's economic salvation does not lie in the amount of money its rich inhabitants can squander recklessly. A nation's economic salvation lies in the amount of money its inhabitants can save and invest after providing themselves with all the necessaries and all the reasonable comforts of life. – R. C. Forbes

The habit of saving is itself an education; it fosters every virtue, teaches self-denial, cultivates the sense of order, trains to forethought, and so broadens the mind. – Theodore T. Munger

When prosperity comes, do not use all of it. – Confucius

Savings represent much more than mere money value. They are the proof that the saver is worth something in himself. Any fool can waste; any fool can muddle; but it takes something more of a man to save and the more he saves the more of a man he makes of himself. Waste and extravagance unsettle a man's mind for every crisis; thrift, which means some form of self-restraint, steadies it. – Rudyard Kipling

All the money in the world is no use to a man or his country if he spends it as fast as he makes it. All he has left is his bills and the reputation for being a fool. – Rudyard Kipling

Save a part of your income and begin now, for the man with a surplus controls circumstances and the man without a surplus is controlled by circumstances. – Henry H. Buckley

A man with a surplus can control circumstances, but a man without a surplus is controlled by them, and often he has no opportunity to exercise judgement. – Harvey S. Firestone

Abstinence from enjoyment is the only source of capital. – Thomas Brassey

Parsimony, and not industry, is the immediate cause of the increase of capital. But whatever industry might acquire, if parsimony did not save and store up, the capital would never be greater. – Adam Smith

Debt

The rich rule over the poor, and the borrower is servant to the lender. – King Solomon (Pr 22:7)

Debt is essentially "spent future income." – Unknown

Never spend your money before you have earned it. – Thomas Jefferson

Once you get into debt, it's hell to get out. Don't let credit card debt carry over. You can't get ahead paying eighteen percent. – Charlie Munger

Capitalism does not exist without capital, and debt is not, has never been and will never be a form of capital. – Ron Paul

Home life ceases to be free and beautiful as soon as it is founded on borrowing and debt. – Henrik Ibseni

Who goeth a borrowing goeth a sorrowing. – Thomas Tusser

A bank is a place where they lend you an umbrella in fair weather and ask for it back when it begins to rain. – Robert Frost

A creditor is worse than a slave owner; for the master owns only your person, but a creditor owns your dignity, and can command it. – Victor Hugo

If we don't discipline ourselves the world will do it for us. – William Feather

I think you should never personally guarantee any debt instrument other than a reasonable mortgage on your home. Real estate is usually financed with some debt, but the property should guarantee it, not your personal signature. – Fred J. Stanback, Jr.

Debt is the worst poverty. – Thomas Fuller

In Aramaic, the word for debt and sin are one and the same...bobha. We have always maintained that carrying too much debt is a slippery slope into financial hell. – William H. Browne, John D. Spears, Robert Q. Wyckoff, Jr., and Thomas H. Shrager

Frugality

One man pretends to be rich, yet has nothing, another pretends to be poor, yet has great wealth. – King Solomon (Pr 13:7)

A man's riches may ransom his life, but a poor man hears no threat. – King Solomon (Pr 13:8)

He who oppresses the poor to increase his wealth and he who gives gifts to the rich— both come to poverty. – King Solomon (Pr 22:16)

It is difficult to set bounds to the price unless you first set bounds to the wish. – Cicero

It is vain to do with more what can be done with less. – William of Occam

To acquire wealth is difficult, to preserve it more difficult, but to spend it wisely most difficult of all. – Edward Day

It's not your salary that makes you rich, it's your spending habits. – Charles A. Jaffe

Beware of little expenses; a small leak will sink a great ship. – Benjamin Franklin

An object in possession seldom retains the same charm that it had in pursuit. – Pliny the Younger

That poverty is no disaster is understood by everyone who has not yet succumbed to the madness of greed and luxury that turns everything topsy-turvy. – Seneca

Frugality includes all the other virtues. – Cicero

We are not to judge thrift solely by the test of saving or spending. If one spends what he should prudently save, that certainly is to be deplored. But if one saves what he should prudently spend, that is not necessarily to be commended. A wise balance between the two is the desired end. – Owen D. Young

A miser grows rich by seeming poor; an extravagant man grows poor by seeming rich. – William Shakespeare

Earn a little, and spend a little—less. – John Stevenson

There must be a reason why some people can afford to live well. They must have worked for it. I only feel angry when I see waste. – Mother Teresa

A man is rich in proportion to the number of things which he can afford to let alone. – Henry David Thoreau

That man is the richest whose pleasures are the cheapest. – Henry David Thoreau

Abundance is, in large part, an attitude. – Sue Patton Thoele

If you wish to make Pythocles rich, do not add to his money, but subtract from his desires. – Epicurus

I am indeed rich, since my income is superior to my expense, and my expense is equal to my wishes. – Edward Gibbon

Food is the most primitive form of comfort. – Sheila Graham

Love what you own, not what you don't. – Unknown

More people should learn to tell their dollars where to go instead of asking them where they went. – Roger W. Babson

Just as soon as people make enough money to live comfortably, they want to live extravagantly. – Author Unknown

Take care of the pennies, and the dollars will take care of themselves. – Jim Lewis

It is not the high cost of living; it is the cost of high living. – Jim Lewis

There is no dignity quite so impressive and no independence quite so important as living within your means. – Calvin Coolidge

In short, the way to wealth, if you desire it, is as plain as the way to market. It depends chiefly on two words, industry and frugality; that is, waste neither time nor money, but make the best use of both. – Benjamin Franklin

If you cannot make money on one dollar—if you do not coax one dollar to work hard for you—you won't know how to make money out of one hundred thousand dollars. – E.S. Kinnear

He who will not economize will have to agonize. – Confucius

Use it up, wear it out, make it do or do without. – Unknown

Making Loans

He who puts up security for another will surely suffer, but whoever refuses to strike hands in pledge is safe. – King Solomon (Pr 11:15)

Do not be a man who strikes hands in pledge or puts up security for debts; if you lack the means to pay, your very bed will be snatched from under you. – King Solomon (Pr 22:26-27)

If you lend money to one of my people among you who is needy, do not treat it like a business deal; charge no interest. – Exodus 22:25

And if you lend to those from whom you expect repayment, what credit is that to you? Even sinners lend to sinners, expecting to be repaid in full. – Luke 6:34

If you lend someone $20 and never see that person again, it was probably a wise investment. – Unknown

It is better to give than to lend, and it costs about the same. – Sir Philip Gibbs

The surest way to ruin a man who doesn't know how to handle money is to give him some. – George Bernard Shaw

If I owe you a pound, I have a problem; but if I owe you a million pounds, you have a problem. – John Maynard Keynes

Investing

It requires a great deal of boldness and a great deal of caution to make a great fortune, and when you have got it, it requires ten times as much wit to keep it. – Ralph Waldo Emerson

Someone who offers to cut you into a successful deal without risk and at little or no charge is likely getting set to con you. – John Train

All these gambling games that are so popular now—commodities, option programs, convertible hedging deals and the like—are not investing at all, and exist to make money for the promoters, not the speculators. – John Train

To trust is good; not to trust is better. – Old Italian Proverb

The best investment is in the tools of one's own trade. – Benjamin Franklin

In investing money, the amount of interest you want should depend on whether you want to eat well or sleep well. – J. Kenfield Morley

Wall Street takes your money and their experience and turns it into their money and your experience. – Unknown

Never ask the barber if you need a haircut. – Warren Buffett

Full-time professionals in other fields, let's say dentists, bring a lot to the layman. But in aggregate, people get nothing for their money from professional money managers. – Warren Buffett

The business schools reward difficult complex behavior more than simple behavior, but simple behavior is more effective. – Warren Buffett

There seems to be some perverse human characteristic that likes to make easy things difficult. – Warren Buffett

Diversification may preserve wealth, but concentration builds wealth. – Warren Buffett

The most important quality for an investor is temperament, not intellect. – Warren Buffett

Success in investing doesn't correlate with IQ once you're above the level of 125. Once you have ordinary intelligence, what you need is the temperament to control the urges that get other people into trouble in investing. – Warren Buffett

I could improve your ultimate financial welfare by giving you a ticket with only twenty slots in it so that you had twenty punches—representing all the investments that you get to make in a lifetime. And once you'd punched through the card, you couldn't make any more investments at all. Under those rules, you'd really think carefully about what you did, and you'd be forced to load up on what you'd really thought about. So you'd do much better. – Warren Buffett

A pin lies in wait for every bubble and when the two eventually meet, a new wave of investors learns some very old lessons. – Warren Buffett

We will reject interesting opportunities rather than over-leverage our balance sheet. – Warren Buffett

If we fear for our physical well being in contemplating a visit to a country, we probably should not invest there. – Chris Browne

It has been my experience that competency in mathematics, both in numerical manipulations and in understanding it's conceptual foundations, enhances a person's ability to handle the more ambiguous and qualitative relationships that dominate our day-to-day financial decision-making. – Alan Greenspan

The individual investor should act consistently as an investor and not as a speculator. This means...that he should be able to justify every purchase he makes and each price he pays by impersonal, objective reasoning that satisfies him that he is getting more than his money's worth for his purchase. – Benjamin Graham

It ain't what you don't know that gets you into trouble. It's what you know for sure that just ain't so. – Mark Twain

Not everything that can be counted counts, and not everything that counts can be counted. – Albert Einstein

The big money is not in the buying and selling...but in the waiting. – Jesse Livermore

The four most expensive words in the English language are, "This time it's different." – Sir John Templeton

Investors have very short memories. – Roman Abramovich

There are huge dangers with computers. People calculate too much and think too little. – Charlie Munger

Our experience tends to confirm a long-held notion that being prepared, on a few occasions in a lifetime, to act promptly in scale, in doing some simple and logical thing, will often dramatically improve the financial results of that lifetime. A few major opportunities, clearly recognizable as such, will usually come to one who continuously searches and waits, with a curious mind that loves diagnosis involving multiple variables. And then all that is required is a willingness to bet heavily when the odds are extremely favorable, using resources available as a result of prudence and patience in the past. – Charlie Munger

Look at those hedge funds—you think they can wait? In my personal portfolio, I have sat for years at a time with $10 to $12 million in treasuries or municipals, just waiting, waiting... – Charlie Munger

It takes character to sit there with all that cash and do nothing. I didn't get to where I am by going after mediocre opportunities. – Charlie Munger

There is no better teacher than history in determining the future...There are answers worth billions of dollars in a $30 history book. – Charlie Munger

The most important thing is for investors to have a realistic idea of what future returns they can look forward to in the stock and bond markets, and not in a day or a week or a month, which is idle and futile, but looking ahead to the next decade and seriously considering what rational expectations might be for market returns. – John Bogle

Time is your friend; impulse is your enemy. – John Bogle

A real estate agent was showing some farmland in a thickly wooded area of North Carolina to a prospective buyer. He pointed to a stream and said, "Why, look at that nice stream over there! Do you realize that if that stream were in Texas, it'd be worth $10,000?" The prospective buyer replied, "Yeah, and if it were in Hell it'd be worth a million." – Tom Stanback

Risk Taking

The Cautious seldom err. – Confucius

Riches do not delight us so much with their possession, as torment us with their loss. – Dick Gregory

We're perfectly willing to trade away a big payoff for a certain payoff. – Warren Buffett

Rule No. 1: Never lose money. Rule No. 2: Never forget rule No. 1. – Warren Buffett

Speculation is the romance of trade, and casts contempt upon all its sober realities. It renders the stock-jobber a magician, and the exchange a region of enchantment. – Washington Irving

When reward is at its pinnacle, risk is near at hand. – John Bogle

There are two times in a man's life when he should not speculate: when he can't afford it, and when he can. – Mark Twain

Making risky investments to get a lot richer will, if they are successful, change the way you can live very little. If they are unsuccessful and you lose a lot of your net worth, it could change your life considerably, both emotionally and practically. – Fred J. Stanback, Jr.

Risk is a combination of consequences and likelihood; if the likelihood is low, then it's easy to think that the risk is low. – Andrew Hopkins

Inflation

Increases in money supply are what constitute inflation, and a general rise in prices is the symptom. – Walter E. Williams

Inflation is a form if hidden taxation, which is almost impossible to measure. – John Beckley

Inflation is the opium of the people. – Henry Hazlitt

Lenin is said to have said the best way to destroy the Capitalist System was to debauch the currency. By a continuing process of inflation, governments can confiscate, secretly and unobserved, an important part of the wealth of their citizens. – John Maynard Keynes

Inflation is taxation without legislation. – Milton Friedman

One of the great defenses if you're worried about inflation is not to have a lot of silly needs in your life—you don't need a lot of material goods. – Charlie Munger

If inflation continues to soar, you're going to have to work like a dog just to live like one. – George Gobel

No civilized country in the world has ever voluntarily adopted the extreme philosophies of either fascism or communism, unless the middle class was first liquidated by inflation. – Henning W. Prentis, Jr.

The arithmetic makes it plain that inflation is a far more devastating tax than anything that has been enacted by our legislature. The inflation tax has a fantastic ability to simply consume capital. It makes no difference to a widow with her savings in a 5 percent passbook account whether she pays 100 percent income tax on her interest income during a period of zero inflation or pays no income taxes during years of 5 percent inflation. Either way, she is 'taxed' in a manner that leaves her no real income whatsoever. Any money she spends comes right out of capital. She would find outrageous a 120 percent income tax, but doesn't seem to notice that 6 percent inflation is the economic equivalent. – Warren Buffett

We believe that our truly urgent need is to make our nation secure, our economy strong and our dollar sound. For every American this matter of the sound dollar is crucial. Without a sound dollar, every American family would face a renewal of inflation, an ever-increasing cost of living, the withering away of savings and life insurance policies. – Dwight D. Eisenhower

Stocks are probably still the best of all the poor alternatives in an era of inflation—at least they are if you buy in at appropriate prices. – Warren Buffett

Businesses with a strong enough competitive position to hike prices can handle rising inflation easily. By contrast, weaker players that can't pass along increases for fear of losing sales have to absorb these costs, putting the squeeze on their profits. – Pat Dorsey

$1 million isn't a lot when measured by its income-producing power, which is something like 2% after inflation and taxes. – Ben Weberman

In an inflationary environment, bond interest is really a taxable return of capital, not spendable income in the old sense. The value of a bond in real terms goes down faster than the income arrives, so if you spend that money you are really invading principal. – John Train

For various reasons, interest on secure corporate bonds in an inflationary situation is rarely as high as the rate of inflation. So if you reinvest all your bond income, not spending a penny, you are still not preserving your capital in real terms, and, of course, taxes make things worse. – John Train

At 5% inflation, $100,000 loses $62,000 of its purchasing power in 20 years. Woe betide the investor who, living in an inflationary economy, treats the interest on bonds or the appreciation on stock as purely spendable money. Spend all your "income" today and you are consuming your capital. Inflation is thus one part of the scissors that are cutting away at capital. The other part is taxes. Since most investors are in or near the top marginal tax rate, a 10% return on stocks or bonds translates into maybe 7% after taxes (less if you live in a high-tax state). Now adjust your return for 5% inflation, and you end with a real return of 2%. Ten percent yields you 2%. – William Baldwin

Stocks

In the short run the market is a voting machine, while in the long run it is a weighing machine. – Benjamin Graham

Most of the time common stocks are subject to irrational and excessive price fluctuations in both directions as the consequence of the ingrained tendency of most people to speculate or gamble...to give way to hope, fear, and greed. – Benjamin Graham

One of the funny things about the stock market is that every time one man buys, another sells, and both think they are astute. – William Feather

Empirical research has shown that 80%-90% of stock returns have occurred in spurts that amount to 2%-7% of the total length of time of the holding period. The rest of the time, stocks' returns have been small. With stocks, your have to "be in it to win it." – William H. Browne, John D. Spears, Robert Q. Wyckoff, Jr., and Thomas H. Shrager

When a hunter looks into the woods, he cannot see the caribou until it moves. After it moves, it seems obvious where the beast had been standing all the time…if investors knew what was going to make the market decline in the future, it would already have declined. – Chris Browne

Market timing would be a wonderful investment tool, if only it worked…instead market peaks and troughs are more like earthquakes. We know they happen, we can even predict with some accuracy where they will happen. We just cannot predict when they will happen. The "when" is what is really important. – Chris Browne

Nothing tells in the long run like a good judgment, and no sound judgment can remain with the man whose mind is disturbed by the mercurial changes of the stock exchange. It places him under an influence akin to intoxication. What is not, he sees, and what he sees, is not. – Andrew Carnegie

When buying shares, ask yourself, "would I buy the whole company?" – Rene Rivkin

Once upon a time in a village, a man appeared and announced to the villagers that he would buy monkeys for $10 each. The villagers, seeing that there were many monkeys around, went out to the forest and started catching them. The man bought thousands at $10 and as supply started to diminish, the villagers stopped their effort. He then announced that he would now buy at $20. This renewed the efforts of the villagers and they started catching monkeys again. Soon the supply diminished even further and people started going back to their farms. The offer increased to $25 each and the supply of monkeys became so little that it was an effort to even see a monkey, let alone catch it! The man now announced that he would buy monkeys at $50! However, since he had to go to the city on some business, his assistant would now buy on behalf of him. In the absence of the man, the assistant told the villagers, "Look at all these monkeys in the big cage that the man has collected. I will sell them to you at $35 and when the man returns from the city, you can sell them to him for $50 each." The villagers rounded up all their savings and bought all the monkeys. But afterwards, they never saw the man nor his assistant again, only monkeys everywhere! Now you have an understanding of how the stock market works. – Unknown

With each investment you make, you should have the courage and the conviction to place at least ten per cent of your net worth in that stock. – Warren Buffett

If a business does well, the stock eventually follows. – Warren Buffett

All there is to investing is picking good stocks at good times and staying with them as long as they remain good companies. – Warren Buffett

Price is what you pay. Value is what you get. – Warren Buffett

The future is never clear, and you pay a very high price in the stock market for a cheery consensus. Uncertainty is the friend of the buyer of long-term values. - Warren Buffett

For some reason, people take their cues from price action rather than from values. What doesn't work is when you start doing things that you don't understand or because they worked last week for somebody else. The dumbest reason in the world to buy a stock is because it's going up. – Warren Buffett

Most people get interested in stocks when everyone else is. The time to get interested is when no one else is. You can't buy what is popular and do well. – Warren Buffett

Be fearful when others are greedy. Be greedy when others are fearful. – Warren Buffett

Never count on making a good sale. Have the purchase price be so attractive that even a mediocre sale gives good results. – Warren Buffett

Investors making purchases in an overheated market need to recognize that it may often take an extended period for the value of even an outstanding company to catch up with the price they paid. – Warren Buffett

If you're an investor, you're looking at what the asset is going to do; if you're a speculator, you're commonly focusing on what the price of the object is going to do, and that's not our game. – Warren Buffett

It's far better to buy a wonderful company at a fair price than a fair company at a wonderful price. – Warren Buffett

Only buy something that you'd be perfectly happy to hold if the market shut down for 10 years. – Warren Buffett

Our favorite holding period is forever. – Warren Buffett

I never attempt to make money on the stock market. I buy on the assumption that they could close the market the next day and not reopen it for five years. – Warren Buffett

Long ago, Sir Isaac Newton gave us three laws of motion, which were the work of genius. But Sir Isaac's talents didn't extend to investing: He lost a bundle in the South Sea Bubble, explaining later, "I can calculate the movement of the stars, but not the madness of men." If he had not been traumatized by this loss, Sir Isaac might well have gone on to discover the Fourth Law of Motion: For investors as a whole, returns decrease as motion increases. – Warren Buffett

If past history was all there was to the game, the richest people would be librarians. – Warren Buffett

We like to buy businesses. We don't like to sell and we expect the relationship to last a lifetime. – Warren Buffett

The stock market serves as a relocation center at which money is moved from the active to the patient. – Warren Buffett

Your goal as an investor should be to purchase, at a rational price, a part interest in an easily-understandable business whose earnings are virtually certain to be materially higher five, ten and twenty years from now. Over time, you will find only a few companies that meet these standards—so when you see one that qualifies, you should buy a meaningful amount of stock. You must also resist the temptation to stray from your guidelines: If you aren't willing to own a stock for ten years, don't even think about owning it for ten minutes. – Warren Buffett

Look at market fluctuations as your friend rather than your enemy; profit from folly rather than participate in it. – Warren Buffett

There's very little money to be made recommending our strategy [buy-and-hold]. Your broker would starve to death. Recommending something to be held for 30 years is a level of self-sacrifice you'll rarely see in a monastery, let alone a brokerage house. – Warren Buffett

Time is the enemy of the poor business and the friend of the great business. – Warren Buffett

The stock market is a no-called-strike game. You don't have to swing at everything—you can wait for your pitch. – Warren Buffett

In the search for companies to acquire, we adopt the same attitude one might find appropriate in looking for a spouse: it pays to be active, interested, and open-minded, but it does not pay to be in a hurry. – Warren Buffett

The strategy we've adopted precludes our following standard diversification dogma. Many pundits would therefore say the strategy must be riskier than that employed by more conventional investors. We disagree. We believe that a policy of portfolio concentration may well decrease risk if it raises, as it should, both the intensity with which an investor thinks about a business and the comfort-level he must feel with it's economic characteristics before buying into it. – Warren Buffett

I put heavy weight on certainty. It's not risky to buy securities at a fraction of what they're worth. – Warren Buffett

We've long felt that the only value of stock forecasters is to make fortune-tellers look good. – Warren Buffett

If you understood a business perfectly and the future of the business, you would need very little in the way of a margin of safety. So, the more vulnerable a business is, assuming you still want to invest in it, the larger margin of safety you'd need. If you're driving a truck across a bridge that says it holds 10,000 pounds and you've got a 9,800 pound vehicle, if the bridge is 6 inches above the crevice it covers, you may feel okay, but if it's over the Grand Canyon, you may feel you want a little larger margin of safety. – Warren Buffett

We have embraced the 21st century by entering such cutting-edge industries as brick, carpet, insulation and paint. Try to control your excitement. – Warren Buffett

If you are a know-something investor, able to understand business economics and to find five to ten sensibly priced companies that possess important long-term competitive advantages, conventional diversification (broadly based active portfolios) makes no sense to you. – Warren Buffett

The professors who taught Efficient Market Theory said that someone throwing darts at the stock tables could select a stock portfolio having prospects just as good as one selected by the brightest, most hard-working securities analyst. Observing correctly that the market was frequently efficient, they went on to conclude incorrectly that it was always efficient. – Warren Buffett

I'd be a bum on the street with a tin cup if the markets were always efficient. – Warren Buffett

The key to investing is not assessing how much an industry is going to affect society, or how much it will grow, but rather determining the competitive advantage of any given company and, above all, the durability of that advantage. – Warren Buffett

I realized that technical analysis didn't work when I turned the chart upside down and didn't get a different answer. - Warren Buffett

Our reaction to a fermenting industry is much like our attitude toward space exploration: we applaud the endeavor but prefer to skip the ride. Obviously many companies in high-tech businesses or embryonic industries will grow much faster than will The Inevitables [like Coca-Cola and Gillette]. But we would rather be certain of a good result than hopeful of a great one. – Warren Buffett

Stocks can't outperform businesses indefinitely. Indeed, because of the heavy transaction and investment management costs they bear, stockholders as a whole and over the long term must inevitably under perform the companies they own. If American business, in aggregate, earns about 12% on equity annually, investors must end up earning significantly less. Bull markets can obscure mathematical laws, but they cannot repeal them. – Warren Buffett

If you understand the business, you don't need to own very many of them. If you have a harem of 40 women, you never get to know any of them very well. – Warren Buffett

Earnings should only be retained [as opposed to being paid out as dividends] when there is a reasonable prospect that for every dollar retained by the corporation, at least one dollar of market value will be created for owners. This will happen only if the capital retained produces incremental earnings equal to, or above, those generally available to investors. – Warren Buffett

The most common cause of low prices is pessimism—sometimes pervasive, sometimes specific to a company or industry. We want to do business in such an environment, not because we like pessimism but because we like the prices it produces. It's optimism that's the enemy of the rational buyer. – Warren Buffett

As far as I am concerned, the stock market doesn't exist. It is only there as a reference to see if anybody is offering to do anything foolish. – Warren Buffett

One of the ironies of the stock market is the emphasis on activity. Brokers, using terms such as "marketability" and "liquidity," sing the praises of companies with high share turnover...but investors should understand that what is good for the croupier is not good for the customer. A hyperactive stock market is the pickpocket of enterprise. – Warren Buffett

I will not abandon a previous approach whose logic I understand (although I find it difficult to apply)—even though it may mean foregoing large, and apparently easy, profits—to embrace an approach which I don't fully understand, have not practiced successfully, and which possibly could lead to substantial permanent loss of capital. – Warren Buffett

There are all kinds of businesses that I don't understand, but that doesn't cause me to stay up at night. It just means I go on to the next one, and that's what the individual investor should do. – Warren Buffett

It has become fashionable at public companies to describe almost every compensation plan as aligning the interests of management with those of shareholders. In our book, alignment means being a partner in both directions, not just on the upside. Many 'alignment' plans flunk this basic test, being artful forms of 'heads I win, tails you lose.' – Warren Buffet

Ben's Mr. Market allegory may seem out-of-date in today's investment world, in which most professionals and academicians talk of efficient markets, dynamic hedging and betas. Their interest in such matters is understandable, since techniques shrouded in mystery clearly have value to the purveyor of investment advice. After all, what witch doctor has ever achieved fame and fortune by simply advising "Take two aspirin"? – Warren Buffett

To be successful, you should concentrate on the world of companies, not arcane accounting mathematics. – Warren Buffett

If you expect to be a net saver during the next 5 years, should you hope for a higher or lower stock market during that period? Many investors get this one wrong. Even though they are going to be net buyers of stocks for many years to come, they are elated when stock prices rise and depressed when they fall. This reaction makes no sense. Only those who will be sellers of equities in the near future should be happy at seeing stocks rise. Prospective purchasers should much prefer sinking prices. – Warren Buffett

Whether we're talking about socks or stocks, I like buying quality merchandise when it is marked down. – Warren Buffett

The new issue market is ruled by controlling stockholders and corporations who can usually select the timing of offerings. Understandably, these sellers are not going to offer any bargains. It's rare you'll find X being sold for half-X. Indeed, in the case of common-stock offerings, selling shareholders are often motivated to unload only when they feel the market is overpaying. – Warren Buffett

A company that wants to use its own stock as currency for an acquisition has no problems if the stock is selling in the market at full intrinsic value. But suppose it is selling at only half intrinsic value. In that case it is faced with the unhappy prospect of using a substantially undervalued currency to pay for a fully valued property [the negotiated price of the target company]. In effect the acquirer must give up $2 of value to receive $1 of value. Under such circumstances, a marvelous business purchased at a fair sales price becomes a terrible buy. For gold valued as gold cannot be purchased intelligently through the utilization of gold valued as lead. – Warren Buffett

If you took our top fifteen decisions out, we'd have a pretty average record. It wasn't hyperactivity, but a hell of a lot of patience. You stuck to your principles and when opportunities came along, you pounced on them with vigor. – Charlie Munger

Go for a business that any idiot can run, because sooner or later, any idiot probably is going to run it. – Peter Lynch

I think you have to learn that there's a company behind every stock, and that there's only one real reason why stocks go up. Companies go from doing poorly to doing well or small companies grow to large companies. – Peter Lynch

When stocks are attractive, you buy them. Sure, they can go lower. I've bought stocks at $12 that went to $2, but then they later went to $30. You just don't know when you can find the bottom. – Peter Lynch

You get recessions. You have stock market declines. If you don't understand that's going to happen, then you're not ready, you won't do well in the markets. – Peter Lynch

Although it's easy to forget sometimes, a share is not a lottery ticket...it's part ownership of a business. – Peter Lynch

I rarely think the market is right. I believe non-dividend stocks aren't much more than baseball cards. They are worth what you can convince someone to pay for it. – Mark Cuban

If you have trouble imaging a 20% loss in the stock market, you shouldn't be in stocks. – John Bogle

The folly of short-term speculation has replaced the wisdom of long-term investing as the star of capitalism. A rent-a-stock system has replaced the earlier own-a-stock system. – John Bogle

The stock market's day-to-day is actually a distraction to the business of investing. – John Bogle

Gold

The great merit of gold is precisely that it is scarce; that its quantity is limited by nature; that it is costly to discover, to mine, and to process; and that it cannot be created by political fiat or caprice. – Henry Hazlitt

A gold mine is a hole in the ground with a liar on top. – Mark Twain

In the absence of the gold standard, there is no way to protect savings from confiscation through inflation. There is no safe store of value. Deficit spending is simply a scheme for the hidden confiscation of wealth. Gold stands in the way of this insidious process. It stands as a protector of property rights. – Alan Greenspan

O Gold! I still prefer thee unto paper, which makes bank credit like a bark of vapour. – Lord Byron

It gets dug out of the ground in Africa, or someplace. Then we melt it down, dig another hole, bury it again and pay people to stand around guarding it. It has no utility. Anyone watching from Mars would be scratching their head. – Warren Buffett

It isn't the gold we have that makes this nation rich. It's what we make, our knowhow, our productivity. So long as this country produces more and better, the world will continue to want what we make. – Malcom Forbes

Two tons of silver and gold coins, hundreds of thousands of nickels, dimes, quarters, and gold pieces. They were under our beds, in the kitchen cupboards, up in the attics, in the bottom of dresser drawers, in holes in the ground. My father was obsessed with gathering up these coins and hiding them away in any likely spot in the houses and garages and store buildings he owned in our tiny town on the mid-Western prairie. Nothing could shake his belief that the total collapse of the American economy and government was just around the corner, a collapse that would bring anarchy and rioting in the streets…In the fairy tale King Midas' daughter was miraculously restored to life after she'd been turned to stone by her father's desire for gold, but Dad's destructive influence on his family could not be so easily reversed. – Alison Johnson

Generosity

A generous man will prosper; he who refreshes others will himself be refreshed. – King Solomon (Pr 11:25)

If a man shuts his ears to the cry of the poor, he too will cry out and not be answered. – King Solomon (Pr 21:13)

He who increases his wealth by exorbitant interest amasses it for another, who will be kind to the poor. – King Solomon (Pr 28:8)

A stingy man is eager to get rich and is unaware that poverty awaits him. – King Solomon (Pr 28:22)

He is not fit for riches who is afraid to use them. – Thomas Fuller

To give away money is an easy matter, and in any man's power. But to decide to whom to give it, and when, and for what purpose and how, is neither in every man's power—nor an easy matter. Hence it is that such excellence is rare, praiseworthy and noble. – Aristotle

If a rich man is proud of his wealth, he should not be praised until it is known how he employs it. – Socrates

There is no gain so certain as that which arises from sparing what you have. – Publilius Syrus

Find out how much God has given you and from it take what you need; the remainder is needed by others. – Saint Augustine

A man there was, and they called him mad; the more he gave, the more he had. – John Bunyan

Make all you can, save all you can, give all you can. – John Wesley

We make a living by what we get, we make a life by what we give. – Winston Churchill

We shall have better business when everyone realizes that while it pays to invest money in their industries and develop natural resources, it pays still higher dividends to improve mankind and develop human resources. – H.E. Steiner

Capital as such is not evil; it is its wrong use that is evil. Capital in some form or other will always be needed. – Mahatma Ghandi

What is most important for democracy is not that great fortunes should not exist, but that great fortunes should not remain in the same hands. In that way they do not form a class. – Alexis De Tocqueville.

Surplus wealth is a sacred trust which its possessor is bound to administer in his lifetime for the good of the community. – Andrew Carnegie

The surplus wealth we have gained to some extent at least belongs to our fellow beings; we are only the temporary custodians of our fortunes, and let us be careful that no just complaint can be made against our stewardship. – Jacob H. Schiff

Rich people should consider that they are only trustees for what they possess, and should show their wealth to be more in doing good than merely in having it. – Joseph Hall

The riches we impart are the only wealth we shall always retain. – Matthew Henry

If you're in the luckiest 1 per cent of humanity, you owe it to the rest of humanity to think about the other 99 per cent. – Warren Buffett

I don't have a problem with guilt about money. The way I see it is that my money represents an enormous number of claim checks on society. It is like I have these little pieces of paper that I can turn into consumption. If I wanted to, I could hire 10,000 people to do nothing but paint my picture every day for the rest of my life. And the GNP would go up. But the utility of the product would be zilch, and I would be keeping those 10,000 people from doing AIDS research, or teaching, or nursing. I don't do that though. I don't use very many of those claim checks. There's nothing material I want very much. And I'm going to give virtually all of those claim checks to charity when my wife and I die. – Warren Buffett

The reaction of my family and me to our extraordinary good fortune is not guilt, but rather gratitude. Were we to use more than 1% of my claim checks on ourselves, neither our happiness nor our well-being would be enhanced. In contrast, that remaining 99% can have a huge effect on the health and welfare of others. That reality sets an obvious course for me and my family: Keep all we can conceivably need and distribute the rest to society, for its needs. – Warren Buffett

Integrity

Like a partridge that hatches eggs it did not lay is the man who gains riches by unjust means. When his life is half gone, they will desert him, and in the end he will prove to be a fool. – Jeremiah 17:11

Ill-gotten treasures are of no value, but righteousness delivers from death. – King Solomon (Pr 10:2)

The wicked man earns deceptive wages, but he who sows righteousness reaps a sure reward. – King Solomon (Pr 11:18)

Misfortune pursues the sinner, but prosperity is the reward of the righteous. – King Solomon (Pr 13:21)

The house of the righteous contains great treasure, but the income of the wicked brings them trouble. – King Solomon (Pr 15:6)

Better a little with righteousness than much gain with injustice. – King Solomon (Pr 16:8)

A greedy man brings trouble on his family, but he who hates bribes will live. – King Solomon (Pr 15:27)

A man of perverse heart does not prosper; he whose tongue is deceitful falls into trouble. – King Solomon (Pr 17:20)

A fortune made by a lying tongue is a fleeting vapor and a deadly snare. – King Solomon (Pr 21:6)

A good name is more desirable than great riches; to be esteemed is better than silver or gold. – King Solomon (Pr 22:1)

Better a poor man whose walk is blameless than a rich man whose ways are perverse. – King Solomon (Pr 28:6)

It is better to be nobly remembered than nobly born. – John Ruskin

With coarse rice to eat, with water to drink, and my bended arm for a pillow—I have still joy in the midst of these things. Riches and honors acquired by unrighteousness are to me as a floating cloud. – Confucius

The superior man understands what is right; the inferior man understands what will sell. – Confucius

It takes 20 years to build a reputation and five minutes to ruin it. If you think about that, you'll do things differently. – Warren Buffett

No man can make good during working hours who does the wrong thing outside of working hours. – William J.H. Boetcker

Money dishonestly acquired is never worth its cost, while a good conscience never costs as much as it is worth. – J.P. Senn

He who wishes to be rich in a day will be hanged in a year. – Leonardo Da Vinci

Knowledge

The wealth of the wise is their crown, but the folly of fools yields folly. – King Solomon (Pr 14:24)

How much better to get wisdom than gold, to choose understanding than silver! – King Solomon (Pr 16:16)

Of what use is money in the hand of a fool, since he has no desire to get wisdom? – King Solomon (Pr 17:16)

He who gets wisdom loves his own soul; he who cherishes understanding prospers. – , King Solomon (Pr 19:8)

Wisdom, like an inheritance, is a good thing and benefits those who see the sun. Wisdom is a shelter as money is a shelter, but the advantage of knowledge is this: Wisdom preserves the life of its possessor. – King Solomon (Ecclesiastes 7:11-12)

I will study and get ready and someday my chance will come. – Abraham Lincoln

Economics or the understanding of money is one of the fundamental skills that are essential for any citizen who aspires to freedom. – John Maynard Keynes

If a man empties his purse into his head, no one can take it away from him. An investment in knowledge always pays the best interest. – Benjamin Franklin

The ideas which now pass for brilliant innovations and advances are in fact mere revivals of ancient errors, and a further proof of the dictum that those who are ignorant of the past are condemned to repeat it. – Henry Hazlitt

Formal education will make you a living; self-education will make you a fortune. – Jim Rohn

I've learned that when a man with money meets a man with experience, the man with the experience ends up with the money and the man with the money ends up with the experience. – Anonymous

Many persons think that by hoarding money they are gaining safety for themselves. If money is your only hope for independence, you will never have it. The only real security that a man can have in this world is a reserve of knowledge, experience and ability. Without these qualities, money is practically useless. The security even of money depends on knowledge, experience and ability. – Henry Ford

If anything is evident about people who manage money, it is that the task attracts a very low level of talent, one that is protected in its highly imperfect profession by the mystery that is thought to enfold the subject of economics in general and of money in particular. – John Kenneth Galbraith

You generally hear that what a man doesn't know doesn't hurt him, but in business what a man doesn't know does hurt. – E.S. Lewis

Though an inheritance of acres may be bequeathed, an inheritance of knowledge and wisdom cannot. The wealthy man may pay others for doing his work for him, but it is impossible to get his thinking done for him by another, or to purchase any kind of self-culture. – Samuel Smiles

A prudent person profits from personal experience, a wise one from the experience of others. – Joseph Collins

It is difficult to get a man to understand something when his salary depends upon his not understanding it. – Upton Sinclair

It is much better to know something about everything than to know everything about one thing. – Blaise Pascal

When you combine ignorance with leverage you get some pretty interesting results. – Warren Buffett

With enough inside information and a million dollars you can go broke in a year. – Warren Buffett

The market, like the Lord, helps those who help themselves. But, unlike the Lord, the market does not forgive those who know not what they do. – Warren Buffett

Priorities and Balance

Do not wear yourself out to get rich; have the wisdom to show restraint. Cast but a glance at riches, and they are gone, for they will surely sprout wings and fly off to the sky like an eagle. – King Solomon (Pr 23:4-5)

For riches do not endure forever, and a crown is not secure for all generations. – King Solomon (Pr 27:24)

Whoever trusts in his riches will fall, but the righteous will thrive like a green leaf. – King Solomon (Pr 11:28)

A faithful man will be richly blessed, but one eager to get rich will not go unpunished. – King Solomon (Pr 28:20)

Prosperity is only an instrument to be used, not a deity to be worshipped. – Calvin Coolidge

He is rich or poor according to what he is, not according to what he has. – Henry Ward Beecher

The true way to gain much is never to desire to gain too much. He is not rich that possesses much, but he that covets no more; and he is not poor that enjoys little, but he that wants too much. – Francis Beaumont

If we command our wealth, we shall be rich and free; if our wealth commands us, we are poor indeed. – Edmund Burke

It is better to live rich than to die rich. – Samuel Johnson

Wealth is a means to an end, not the end itself. As a synonym for health and happiness, it has had a fair trial and failed dismally. – John Galsworthy

If you want to hear about the power and glory of wealth, ask a man who's seeking it. But if you want to learn of wealth's burdens and difficulties, ask a man who's been wealthy a long time. – Stanley Goldstein

If you want to feel rich, just count the things you have that money can't buy – Unknown

No one can serve two masters. Either you will hate the one and love the other, or you will be devoted to the one and despise the other. You cannot serve both God and money. – Matthew 6:24

For the love of money is a root of all kinds of evil. Some people, eager for money, have wandered from the faith and pierced themselves with many griefs. – The Apostle Paul (1 Timothy 6:10)

Money is a terrible master but an excellent servant. – P.T. Barnum

Money never made a man happy yet, nor will it. The more a man has, the more he wants. Instead of filling a vacuum, it makes one. – Benjamin Franklin

Leisure is time for doing something useful, and this leisure the diligent man will obtain. – Benjamin Franklin

The use of money is all the advantage there is in having money. – Benjamin Franklin

He who is of the opinion that money will do everything may well be suspected of doing everything for money. – Benjamin Franklin

The be-all and end-all of life should not be to get rich, but to enrich the world. – B.C. Forbes

Earth provides enough to satisfy every man's need, but not every man's greed. – Mahatma Gandhi

Riches prick us with a thousand troubles in getting them, as many cares in preserving them, and yet more anxiety in spending them, and with grief in losing them. – Saint Francis

You were intended not only to work, but to rest, laugh, play and have proper leisure and enjoyment. To develop an all-around personality you must have interest outside of your regular vocation that will serve to balance your business responsibilities. – Grenville Kleiser

Recreation is but a change of work—an occupation for the hands by those who live by their brains, or for the brains by those who live by their hands. – Dorothy Thompson

Every now and then go away, have a little relaxation, for when you come back to your work your judgment will be surer, since to remain constantly at work will cause you to lose power of judgment. Go some distance away, because then the work appears smaller, and more of it can be taken in at a glance, and lack of harmony and proportion is more readily seen. – Leonardo Da Vinci

If your business keeps you so busy that you have no time for anything else, there must be something wrong, either with you or with your business. – William J.H. Boetcker

Too often, a vast collection of possessions ends up possessing its owner. The asset I most value, aside from health, is interesting, diverse, and long-standing friends. – Warren Buffett

Money, to some extent, sometimes lets you be in more interesting environments. But it can't change how many people love you or how healthy you are. – Warren Buffett

Many possessions, if they do not make a man better, are at least expected to make his children happier; and this pathetic hope is behind many exertions. – Karl Wilhelm Von Humboldt

It is preoccupation with possessions, more than anything else, that prevents us from living freely and nobly. – Henry David Thoreau

That anyone should be able to make it the sole purpose of his life-work, to sink into the grave weighed down with a great material load of money and goods, seems explicable only as the product of a perverse imagination. – Max Weber

Possessions, outward success, publicity, luxury—to me these have always been contemptible. I believe that a simple and unassuming manner of life is best for everyone, best both for the body and the mind. – Albert Einstein

People who cannot find time for recreation are obliged sooner or later to find time for illness. – John Wanamaker

Money and Relationships

A friendship founded on business is a good deal better than a business founded on friendship. – John D. Rockefeller

Lots of people want to ride with you in the Limo, but what you want is someone who will take the bus with you when the Limo breaks down. – Oprah Winfrey

Anyone who marries for money earns every cent of it. – Unknown

Don't marry for money. You can borrow it cheaper. – Unknown

Of all the icy blasts that blow on love, a request for money is the most chilling and havoc-wreaking. – Gustave Flaubert

Money will buy you a bed, but not a good night's sleep, a house but not a home, a companion but not a friend. – Zig Ziglar

I believe that being successful means having a balance of success stories across the many areas of your life. You can't truly be considered successful in your business life if your home life is in shambles. – Zig Ziglar

Paying Taxes

Keeping a close watch on him, they sent spies, who pretended to be honest. They hoped to catch Jesus in something he said so that they might hand him over to the power and authority of the governor. So the spies questioned him: "Teacher, we know that you speak and teach what is right, and that you do not show partiality but teach the way of God in accordance with the truth. Is it right for us to pay taxes to Caesar or not?" He saw through their duplicity and said to them, "Show me a denarius. Whose portrait and inscription are on it?" "Caesar's," they replied. He said to them, "Then give to Caesar what is Caesar's, and to God what is God's." – Luke 20-25

Why shouldn't the American people take half my money from me? I took all of it from them. – Edward A. Filene

The point to remember is what the government gives it must first take away. – John S. Coleman

I like to pay taxes. With them I buy civilization. – Oliver Wendell Holmes

When you want something, you have to be willing to pay your dues. – Les Brown

Taxes are not good things, but if you want services, somebody's got to pay for them so they're a necessary evil. – Michael Bloomberg

Each citizen contributes to the revenues of the State a portion of his property in order that his tenure of the rest may be secure. – Baron De Montesquieu

When everybody has got money they cut taxes, and when they're broke they raise taxes. That's statesmanship of the highest order. – Will Rogers

Taxes are paid in the sweat of every man who labors. If those taxes are excessive, they are reflected in idle factories, tax-sold farms and in hordes of hungry people, tramping the streets and seeking jobs in vain. – Franklin D. Roosevelt

We contend that for a nation to try to tax itself into prosperity is like a man standing in a bucket and trying to lift himself up by the handle. – Winston Churchill

Taxes are usually underpaid out of intent, but overpaid out of ignorance. – James L. Halperin and Gregory J. Rohan

Trying to minimize taxes too much is one of the great standard causes of really dumb mistakes. – Charlie Munger

Wall Street invents an ever-changing series of complicated products to make commissions and fees for themselves. Usually these have some "tax saving" angle. Most of them make no sense for most investors. But if they don't sell them, their children don't eat. – Fred J. Stanback, Jr.

Inheritances

A good man leaves an inheritance for his children's children, but a sinner's wealth is stored up for the righteous. – King Solomon (Pr 13:22)

An inheritance quickly gained at the beginning will not be blessed at the end. – King Solomon (Pr 20:21)

That which we acquire with the most difficulty we retain the longest; as those who have earned a fortune are usually more careful of it than those who have inherited one. – Charles Caleb Colton

A man who gives his children habits of industry provides for them better than by giving them a fortune. – Richard Whatley

A very rich person should leave his kids enough to do anything but not enough to do nothing. – Warren Buffett